Collection

ıgawa

Saxy Ever"

須川展也サクソフォン＝コレクション

Chick Corea
Florida to Tokyo
Sonata for alto saxophone and piano

チック・コリア
Florida to Tokyo
アルト・サクソフォンとピアノのためのソナタ

ZEN-ON MUSIC

Sonata for Alto Saxophone and Piano "Florida to Tokyo"

"I someday wish for Maestro Chick Corea to compose a piece for classical saxophonists in the world!" Believe it or not, that dream came true. *Sonata for Alto Saxophone and Piano "Florida to Tokyo"*. An exquisite piece of music delivered from Florida to Tokyo, and into the world, is born. Maestro Chick Corea caring of classical saxophone, wrote down all notes in detail, and presented me with a wonderful piece.

Maestro Chick Corea is the master of jazz world, however has also composed classical pieces (such as "Children's Songs" and "Lyric Suite for Sextet"). I have been a big fan of his "Spain" and " La Fiesta", that I have performed them many times in my concert, and have strongly been attracted to his classical style music for a long time.

Yearning for a composed piece someday, I finally had the opportunity to be introduced to Maestro Chick Corea through a jazz pianist and composer, Mr. Ken Shima, and I directly expressed my feelings to Maestro.

The piece begins from a music dialogue between the piano and saxophone, and with Maestro's musical language, it develops as if narrating history of music. A single movement of approximately 13 minutes. It is a free sonata, as it means from the very beginning "a piece played".

Direction says that dynamics, articulation, and nuance, would be up to the performer, however the carefully selected notes in the score feel like they are all narrating.

*There is another direction as the end of the piece, that the extremely high note may be an octave lower.

Nobuya Sugawa

(Translated by Aya Yamagishi)

Commissioned by Nobuya Sugawa

The world premiere : October 15, 2016, at Dai-Ichi Seimei Hall (Tokyo)

　　　　　　　Nobuya Sugawa (Alto Saxophone) and Minako Koyanagi (Piano)

CD : "Nobuya Sugawa: Masterpieces" (YCCS-10059),

　　　recorded by Nobuya Sugawa (Alto Saxophone) and Minako Koyanagi (Piano)

Duration : approximately 13 minutes 30 seconds

*Two kinds of parts attached in this publication: (1) Original version by Chick Corea and (2) Edited version by Nobuya Sugawa. And the original one is written in the piano score.

アルト・サクソフォンとピアノのためのソナタ "Florida to Tokyo"

『いつかチック・コリアさんに、世界のクラシカル・サクソフォン奏者のために曲を書いていただきたい！』
なんとその夢が叶いました。
Sonata for Alto Saxophone and Piano "Florida to Tokyo"
フロリダから東京へ、そしてさらに世界に伝わる名曲の誕生です。
チック・コリアさんがクラシカル・サクソフォンを想い、さらに全ての音を細かく書き記し、素晴らしい曲を贈ってくださいました。
ジャズ界の巨匠であるチック・コリアさんですが、クラシカルな作品（「チルドレンズ・ソング」や「セクステットのための叙情組曲」等）も作曲されています。
私はもともとチック・コリアさんの「スペイン」や「ラ・フィエスタ」の大ファンで、これまでに何度も自分のコンサートで演奏してきましたが、チック・コリアさんのクラシック・スタイルの曲にもずっと強く惹かれていたのです。
いつか曲を書いていただきたい、という想いが募り、ついにジャズ・ピアニスト＆作曲家の島健さんにチック・コリアさんをご紹介いただき、その気持ちを直接ご本人に伝えました。
曲は、ピアノとサックスの音楽の会話から始まり、チック・コリアさんの音楽語法により、まるで音楽の歴史を語るように展開していきます。13分ほどの単一楽章。「演奏されるもの」という元々の意味通りの、自由なソナタです。強弱、アーティキュレーション、ニュアンスなどは奏者にお任せ、との指示がありますが、譜面に描かれている吟味された音の全てが、まるで語りかけるようです。
※曲の最後に、サクソフォンの超高音がありますが、オクターブ下で吹いても構わないとの指示もあり。

須川　展也

委嘱：須川展也
初演：2016年10月15日、第一生命ホール（東京）
　　　須川展也（アルト・サクソフォン）、小柳美奈子（ピアノ）
CD：「須川展也　Masterpieces」（YCCS-10059）［演奏：須川展也（アルト・サクソフォン）、小柳美奈子（ピアノ）］
演奏所要時間：約13分30秒

※本出版物の付属パート譜には作曲者オリジナル版と須川展也校訂版の2種類があり、ピアノ・スコア中では前者のみを掲載しています。

Florida to Tokyo

Sonata for Alto Saxophone and Piano

Chick Corea

Cadenza – free time

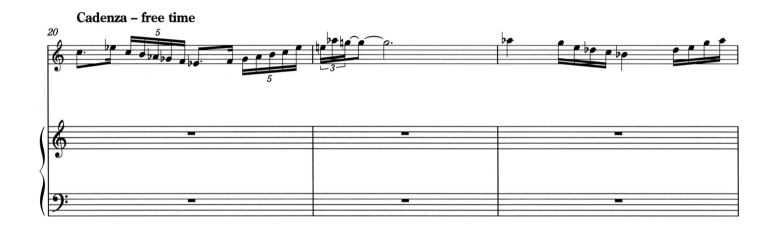

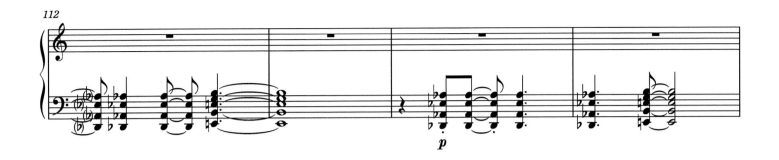

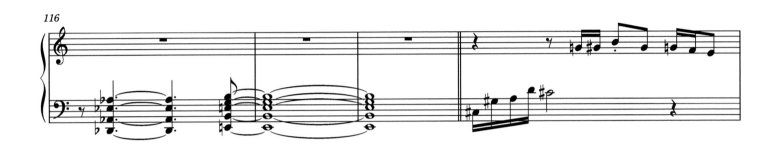

Alto Saxophone in E♭

[Edited by Nobuya Sugawa*]

Florida to Tokyo

Sonata for Alto Saxophone and Piano

Chick Corea

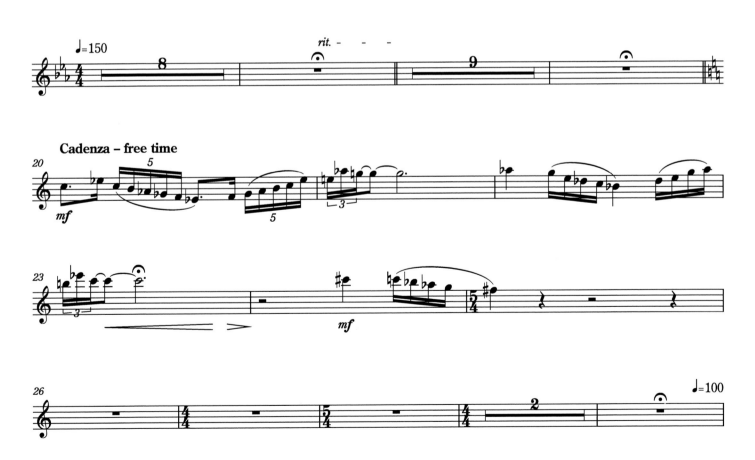

*Dynamics and articulation which are not in the composer's Original version are added by Nobuya Sugawa.

5

Alto Saxophone in E♭

[Original Version by Chick Corea*]

Florida to Tokyo

Sonata for Alto Saxophone and Piano

Chick Corea

*Dynamics, articulation, and nuance, would be up to the performer.

5

Alto Sax Cadenza – free time >>

free time (rubato)

12

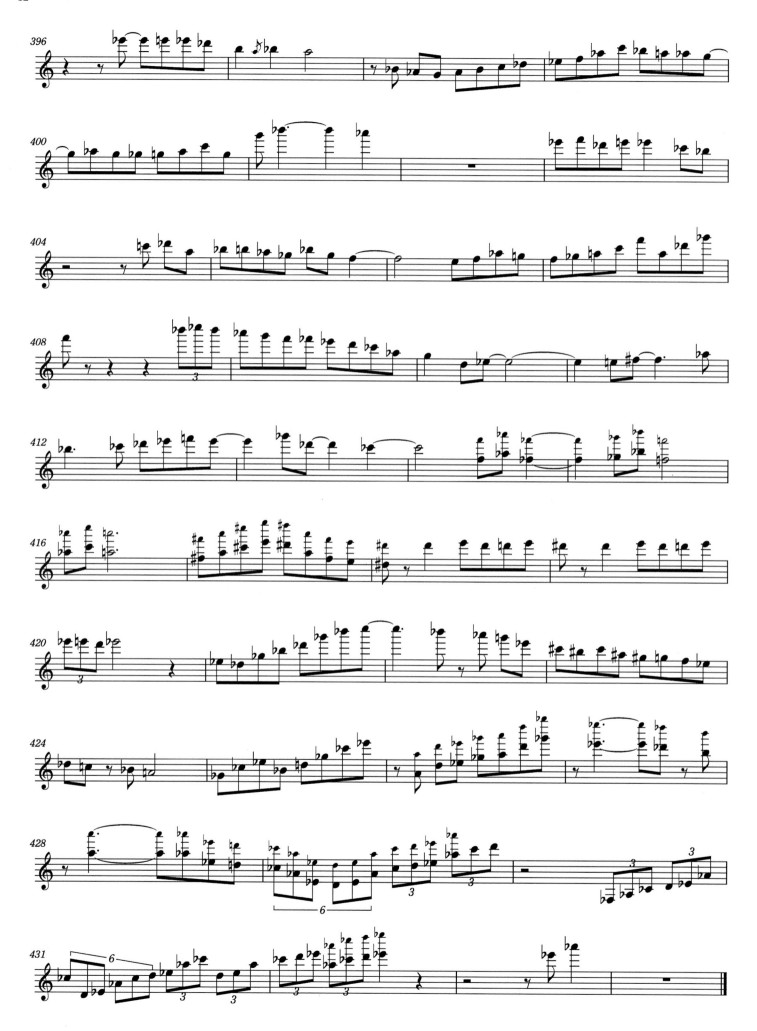

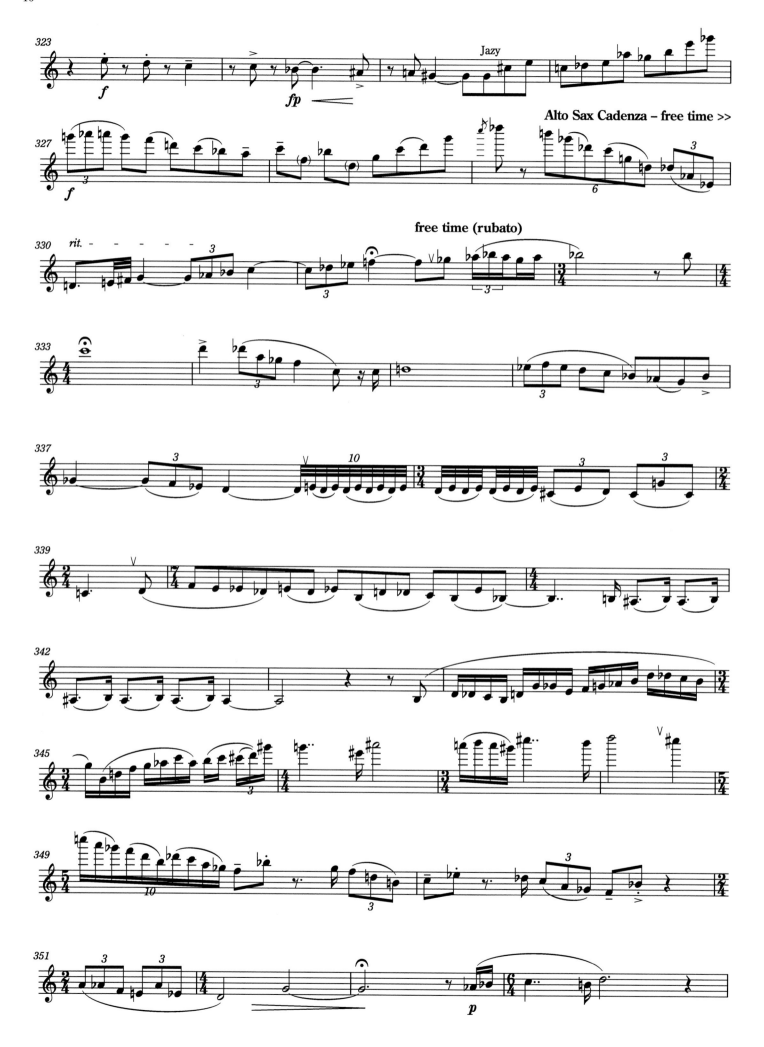

須川展也サクソフォン=コレクション　Collection Nobuya Sugawa "Saxy Ever"

オリジナル編（SEO）Originals

番号 No.	作曲者 Composer	作品 Title	編成 Instrumentation
SEO-001	西村 朗 Akira Nishimura	ラメント Lamento	a.sax/pft
SEO-002	佐藤 聰明 Sômei Satoh	ランサローテ Lanzarote	s.sax or cl/pft
SEO-003	長生 淳 Jun Nagao	天国の月 La lune en paradis	a.sax/pft
SEO-004	Cl. ドビュッシー Cl.Debussy	ラプソディ Rapsodie	a.sax/pft
SEO-005	本多 俊之・尚美 Toshiyuki and Naomi Honda	ジャズ・エチュード Jazz etude	s&a.sax/pft
SEO-006	鍋島 佳緒里 Kaori Nabeshima	エキゾティック・ダンス Exotic dance	a.sax/pft
SEO-007	小六 禮次郎 Reijiro Koroku	SAKURA SAKURA	s&a.sax/pft
SEO-008	長生 淳 Jun Nagao	サクソフォン四重奏曲 Quatuor de Saxophones	s.a.t.b.sax
SEO-009	金子 仁美 Hitomi Kaneko	気泡 La bulle	a.sax/pft
SEO-010	加羽沢 美濃 Mino Kabasawa	黒い森/S・N・S Schwarzwald/S・N・S	a.sax/pft
SEO-011	久留 智之 Tomoyuki Hisatome	メリー・バクテリア・ミュージック Merry Bacteria Music	a.sax/fl.&picc.
SEO-012	R. ヴィードフ R. Wiedoeft	コンサート曲集 Concert Pieces	a.sax/pft
SEO-013	長生 淳 Jun Nagao	彗星 トルヴェールの《遊星》より Comets from "The Planets" by Trouvère	s.a.t.b.sax
SEO-014	池辺 晋一郎（詩：池澤夏樹） Shin-ichiro Ikebe (Poem: Natsuki Ikezawa)	軌道エレベーター The Orbit Elevator	s.&a.sax/voice
SEO-015	長生 淳 Jun Nagao	天頂の恋 Lovers on the Celestial Sphere	s.t.sax/pft
SEO-016	長生 淳 Jun Nagao	Shall We Sax? Shall We Sax?	s.a.t.b.sax
SEO-017	北爪 道夫 Michio Kitazume	チェーン Chain	s.sax
SEO-018	長生 淳 Jun Nagao	パガニーニ・ロスト Paganini Lost	a.a.sax/pft
SEO-019	加藤 昌則 Masanori Katoh	オリエンタル Oriental	s.a.sax/pft
SEO-020	西村 朗 Akira Nishimura	水の影 Water Shadows	a.sax
SEO-021	新実 徳英 Tokuhide Niimi	サクソフォン・スパイラル Saxophone Spiral	a.a.sax
SEO-022	池辺 晋一郎 Shin-ichiro Ikebe	バイヴァランスⅧ Bivalence VIII	s.&a.sax/t.&b.sax
SEO-023	加藤 昌則 Masanori Katoh	スロヴァキアン・ラプソディ Slovakian Rhapsody	a.sax/pft
SEO-024	長生 淳 Jun Nagao	ラフォリスム L'aphorisme	s.sax/pft
SEO-025	石川 亮太 Ryota Ishikawa	日本民謡による狂詩曲 Rhapsody on Japanese Folk Songs	a.sax/pft
SEO-026	新実 徳英 Tokuhide Niimi	ラ・ヴァルス F La Valse F	a.sax/pft
SEO-027	加藤 昌則 Masanori Katoh	ソナタ・ルシーダ Sonata Lùcida	a.sax/pft
SEO-028	チック・コリア ChickCorea	Florida to Tokyo Florida to Tokyo	a.sax/pft
SEO-029	西村 朗 Akira Nishimura	ハラーハラ Halahala	a.sax

アレンジ編（SEA）Arrangements

番号 No.	作曲者 Composer	作品 Title	編成 Instrumentation
SEA-001	C. ガルデル／啼鵬 C.Gardel / Têhô	想いの届く日 El dia que me quieras	a.sax/pft
SEA-002	M. ポンセ／朝川 朋之 M.Ponce / T.Asakawa	エストレリータ Estrellita	a.sax/pft
SEA-003	A. ピアソラ／啼鵬 A.Piazzolla / Têhô	アディオス・ノニーノ Adios nonino	a.sax/pft
SEA-004	A. ララ／森田 一浩 A.Lara / K. Morita	グラナダ Granada	a.sax/pft
SEA-005	R. シューマン／須川 展也 R.Schumann / N. Sugawa	アダージョとアレグロ Adagio and Allegro	s.or t.sax/pft
SEA-006	M. ラヴェル／須川 展也 M.Ravel / N. Sugawa	亡き王女のためのパヴァーヌ Pavane pour une infante défunte	s.(t.) or a.(b.)sax/pft
SEA-007	G. ガーシュウィン／長生 淳 G.Gershwin / J. Nagao	ラプソディー・イン・ブルー Rhapsody in Blue	s.a.t.sax/pft
SEA-008	M. ムソルグスキー／長生 淳 M.Mussorgsky / J. Nagao	展覧会の絵 Pictures at an Exhibition	s.a.t.b.sax/pft
SEA-009	G. プッチーニ／須川 展也 G.Puccini / N. Sugawa	誰も寝てはならぬ オペラ（トゥーランドット）より Nessun dorma! from opera "Turandot"	s.(t.) or a.(b.)sax/pft
SEA-010	V. ベッリーニ／須川 展也 V.Bellini / N. Sugawa	清らかな女神よ オペラ（ノルマ）より Casta Diva from opera "Norma"	s.(t.) or a.(b.)sax/pft
SEA-011	S. ラフマニノフ／須川 展也 S.Rachmaninoff / N. Sugawa	ヴォカリーズ Vocalise	s.(t.) or a.(b.)sax/pft
SEA-012	C. サン=サーンス／須川 展也 C.Saint-Saëns / N. Sugawa	白鳥 Le Cygne	s.(t.) or a.(b.)sax/pft
SEA-013	C. グノー／須川 展也 C.Gounod / N. Sugawa	アヴェ・マリア Ave Maria	s.(t.) or a.(b.)sax/pft
SEA-014	G. ガーシュウィン／伊藤 康英 G.Gershwin / Y. Ito	サマータイム Summertime	s.(t.) or a.(b.)sax/pft
SEA-015	G. ガーシュウィン／伊藤 康英 G.Gershwin / Y. Ito	バイ・シュトラウス By Strauss	s.(t.) or a.(b.)sax/pft
SEA-016	G. カッチーニ／朝川 朋之 G.Caccini / T. Asakawa	アヴェ・マリア Ave Maria	a.sax/pft

チック・コリア：Florida to Tokyo ●

作曲	チック・コリア
監修	須川展也
第1版第1刷発行	2019年4月15日
第1版第2刷発行	2019年6月 5日
発行	株式会社全音楽譜出版社
	東京都新宿区上落合2丁目13番3号 〒161-0034
	TEL・営業部 03・3227-6270
	出版部 03・3227-6280
	URL　http://www.zen-on.co.jp/
	ISBN978-4-11-560028-7

19050127

日本音楽著作権協会（JASRAC）（ジャスラック）（出）許諾1903439-902号
（許諾番号の対象は、当該出版物中、当協会が許諾することのできる著作物に限られます。）